Dilly

BREAKS THE RULES

DILLY

BREAKS THE RULES

TONY BRADMAN

ILLUSTRATED BY SUSAN HELLARD

mammoth

For Eloïse

T.B.

First published in Great Britain in 1999 by Mammoth
an imprint of Egmont Children's Books Limited
239 Kensington High Street, London W8 6SA

Text copyright © 1999 Tony Bradman
Illustrations copyright © 1999 Susan Hellard

The moral rights of the author and illustrator have been asserted.

The rights of Tony Bradman and Susan Hellard to be
identified as the author and illustrator of this work have
been asserted by them in accordance with the
Copyright, Designs and Patents Act 1988

ISBN 0 7497 3828 6

10 9 8 7 6 5 4 3 2

A CIP catalogue record for this book is
available from the British Library

Printed in Great Britain by Cox & Wyman Ltd,
Reading, Berkshire

Contents

1 Dilly goes to big school

'Come on, Dorla, cheer up,' said Mother as we walked down the street in the morning sunshine. 'It's not like you to be miserable on the first day of term! Usually you can't wait to get back to school after the holidays.'

'That's because it usually means I'm escaping from Dilly,' I muttered. The pest in question was skipping along ahead of us with Father, as happy as could be. 'And I won't be able to do that after today – will I?'

I'd spent most of the summer trying hard not to think about it, but it was all too true. Dilly had been at Mrs Dactyl's nursery for the last couple of years.

This term, however, he was finally moving on to big school.

My pain of a little brother was going to be in the same school as me, and I dreaded it. Not just because it meant I'd be seeing a lot more of him, although that was bad enough. No, there was something much worse.

Everybody where we live knows Dilly. Our neighbours, and grown-ups who work at places like the Shopping Cavern and the Swamp, often refer to me as *Dilly's big sister*. I haven't told Mother and Father, but I loathe it.

Now Dilly was invading the one place it didn't happen. The one place I had always been ... *Dorla*, and not just the sister of a badly behaved brat.

'Relax, Dorla,' said Mother, as we reached the crowd of dinosaurs at the school gate, and caught up with Father and Dilly. 'You never know – the two of you being here together might turn out to be a good thing.'

'Oh, yeah,' I said. 'And brontosauruses might fly.'

'We can do without the smart remarks, Dorla,'

said Father, sternly. 'What your mother means is that we were hoping you two might make more of an effort to get along. Now you're in the same school, that is.'

I could hardly believe my ears. I glanced at Dilly, and Dilly glanced at me, then we both gave our parents a silent, withering And-What-Planet-Are-You-Living-On? stare. Sometimes I wonder about them, I really do.

'Well, you might at least look out for your little brother to begin with, Dorla,' said Mother. Father nodded, and kept nodding as she continued. 'Er . . . you could show him the ropes, make sure he's coping all right . . .'

'Forget it,' said Dilly. 'I need *her*,' he added, snootily pointing his snout in my direction, 'like I need a spare tail. I can look out for myself. I'll be fine, Mother and Father. In fact, I think big school is going to be . . . terrific.'

'Suits me,' I snapped. 'Once we're through the school gate, he's on his own,' I said, snootily pointing my snout in *his* direction. 'And he'd better remember not to come running to me for help when things go wrong.'

Then we both gave a loud SNIFF! and turned our backs on each other.

'Family life,' muttered Father, rolling his eyes and sighing deeply. 'Don't you just love it? OK, I think we ought to get these two into school before I lose my temper with them. This way, please – left, right, left, right, left . . .'

And with that, he marched us into the playground. I saw my friends, and said goodbye to Mother and Father. Then they took Dilly inside to his new teacher, Mrs Dapple. She had been my first teacher at big school, too.

I'd already told Dilly he was very lucky to start

off with Mrs Dapple. I'd loved being in her class, and I know she's always liked me. She stops to chat when ever we meet in the corridor, and asks how I'm doing.

I kept telling myself I didn't care what Dilly was doing that day, but it wasn't true. Even though I was busy getting used to being in my new class, I still did plenty of worrying about what he might be up to.

I didn't see him again until assembly. Mrs Dapple led her class into the hall, and Dilly came dawdling way behind the others. Mrs Dapple said something to him, but I was too far away to hear what it was.

I did notice that Dilly suddenly began scowling, though.

'Well, Dilly,' said Mother with a smile when she and Father came to collect us that afternoon. 'We didn't get a phone call, Mrs Dapple hasn't resigned, and the school is still standing . . . I take it you had a good day.'

'It was . . . OK,' said Dilly, rather grumpily. 'Can we go home now?'

Mother and Father asked Dilly lots of questions as we drove towards our house, and he didn't give them many answers. He wasn't quite as grumpy by the time we sat down to eat dinner, but he didn't want to talk.

'He's probably just tired,' I overheard Mother saying to Father later, after they'd put Dilly to bed. I was in my room, and I sneaked a peek at them round my door. 'I'm certain he'll soon settle in,' Mother added.

I wasn't so sure, especially after what I'd seen earlier that day. And judging by the way Mother touched wood on the banisters as she went downstairs, and Father had his tail crossed, neither were our parents.

Dilly seemed all right in the morning, if a bit

quiet. Mother and Father took us to school, and I didn't really see much of Dilly until home time. But the moment I set eyes on him at the gate, I knew he wasn't happy.

'So, did you have a good day today, Dorla?' Father asked me when we climbed into the dino-car. I said I did. 'And, er . . .what about you, Dilly?'

'Huh!' snorted Dilly, even more grumpily than before. He strapped himself in his seat, folded his arms, and scowled darkly. 'No comment.'

Of course, Mother and Father instantly plunged into Worried-Parent-Mode and, when we got home, they gave Dilly the old Tell-Us-What's-Wrong-And-We'll-Sort-It-Out line. But his lips remained firmly sealed.

'OK, have it your way, Dilly,' sighed Mother eventually. 'But I think we'll come and have a word with Mrs Dapple if you don't settle in by the end of the week. We can't have you not enjoying school now, can we?'

Dilly just trudged upstairs, TRUDGE, TRUDGE, TRUDGE, then shut his bedroom door with a . . . SLAM! Mother and Father winced in unison.

They were even more worried now – but I was intrigued. This simply wasn't like Dilly. When he gets upset, he usually lets everybody know why – very soon, and very loudly. It was time to do some investigating.

The next morning I went into the main school building by a different entrance from normal, one which would take me through the cloakroom Mrs Dapple's class used. I got there just as Dilly was hanging up his coat.

Or rather, I should say . . . just as he threw it in the general direction of his hanger. It missed completely, and fell on the floor – but, as you would expect, Dilly wasn't bothered. He turned and made for his classroom.

'Oh, deary me, *that* won't do,' said a voice I

recognised. I slipped into the shadows as Mrs Dapple tutted, turned Dilly round, and sent him back. 'I would have expected Dorla's little brother to be *much* tidier,' she added.

I couldn't see Dilly's face from where I stood, but when Mrs Dapple said 'Dorla's little brother' his body went rigid. He paused for a second, then he scooped up his coat ... and placed it *very* carefully on the hanger.

Once I started listening for them, I heard Mrs Dapple use those same three words a lot that day. 'I wouldn't have expected *Dorla's little brother* to do that,' she would say. And, quite obviously, Dilly . . . loathed it.

He clearly didn't want to tell our parents either, and he couldn't ask me for help – even though he knew I knew. He spotted me hiding behind a bookshelf, eavesdropping as Mrs Dapple compared him to me yet again. If looks could kill, I would have been vapourised. I gave him a Serves-You-Right glare and walked away. But I was rather surprised to discover I wasn't as pleased Dilly was having a bad time as I thought I would be . . .

The problem was – I knew *exactly* how he felt. I sat brooding in class that afternoon, trying hard to convince myself it was none of my business. Then I slowly began to realise I wouldn't wish those feelings on *anybody*. Not my worst enemy . . . not even my total pain of a little brother.

Suddenly, in the distance, I heard the unmistakable sound of an ultra-special, 150-mile-per-hour super-scream, the  kind that makes floors and walls shake, and windows rattle, and classroom doorknobs PING! off.

Dilly's patience had snapped at last.

One of Dilly's classmates came to fetch me. Mother and Father had been summoned by phone, and Mrs Dapple wanted me to try to calm Dilly down while she waited for them. He was very, very upset.

'I simply don't understand it,' murmured a trembling Mrs Dapple, who was pretty upset herself. 'I wouldn't have expected your little brother . . .'

'I think that's actually the trouble, Miss,' I said. Dilly stopped sobbing and glanced round. 'You keep calling him that – and he doesn't like it.'

'Oh deary me!' said Mrs Dapple, a green flush creeping up her neck.

Dilly stared at me with his mouth open for a second, then came over, slipped his paw into mine, and squeezed. I gently squeezed back.

Mrs Dapple seemed terribly embarrassed, so I could tell she knew I was right. When Mother and Father arrived, Mrs Dapple immediately said everything was her fault, and promised Dilly she would make a fresh start.

She did, too. In fact, she got the Head to make a rule that *nobody* at our school should be referred to as somebody's brother or sister. I told Mother and Father I thought that should be the rule everywhere . . . and they agreed.

So maybe things will be improving in our neighbourhood, too.

'Well, there you are,' said Mother at the gate the day we heard about the new rule. Dilly was settling in at last, and getting on fine with Mrs Dapple. 'You two being in the same school *has* turned out to be a good thing.'

'Hey, look!' said Father, pointing skywards. 'A flying brontosaurus!'

'Oh, very funny, Father,' said Dilly. 'I *don't* think.'

But we all laughed, just the same. And then we went home for tea . . .

2 Dilly and the missing pet

'I wish I'd never applied for that job now,' muttered Mother as she paced anxiously up and down the sitting-room. 'I don't know why they're even bothering to give me an interview. I'm certain it's going to be a *disaster*.'

Mother had been like this for the last couple of days, ever since she'd had the letter about her interview. It wasn't actually due to take place until the following week, but the closer it got, the more nervous she became.

'You think *you've* got problems!' said Father, who was sitting on the sofa surrounded by lists and plans. 'It's only a month till the summer fair, and there's simply no *way* I'll have everything sorted out by then!'

Father wasn't particularly happy either. The PTA committee at our school had asked him to organise this year's summer fair, and he'd agreed. But it had turned out to be a lot more difficult than he'd thought.

I had a few worries myself, too. I'd been made captain of my year's tail-ball team, and I had begun to wonder whether I could handle the pressure. I was just about to join the conversation . . . but then Dilly walked in.

He took no notice of the three of us. He padded slowly round the room, peered behind the TV, lay flat on the floor to look under the sofa and chairs, stood up again, then headed for the door, all without a single word.

'Er . . . hang on a minute, Dilly,' said Mother, moving to block his path. 'Would you mind telling us exactly what you're doing? Call me crazy, but seeing you behave strangely always makes me feel uncomfortable.'

'I'm looking for Swampy, Mother,' Dilly replied in his serious voice. 'And I can't seem to find him. You don't know where he is, do you?'

Dilly thinks the world of his pet swamp lizard. Swampy is pretty fond of Dilly as well, and they're usually inseparable, although Swampy does have a habit of wandering off on his own sometimes for a sleep.

So Dilly having to search for him wasn't out of the ordinary.

'I'm sorry, Dilly, I don't,' she said. 'Do you, dear?'

'Haven't got a clue, I'm afraid,' said Father. 'Dorla?'

'Me neither,' I said, and shrugged.

'But I *have* to find him,' said Dilly, a note of desperation in his voice.

'OK, Dilly, stay calm,' said Mother with a sigh.

'Luckily, there's one infallible method of solving this particular problem. Follow me.'

I went too. Mother led Dilly to the kitchen and got a can of Swampy's favourite food out of the cupboard. She opened it, dolloped some in Swampy's bowl, and banged on the side with the spoon she'd used.

'Swampy!' she yelled at the top of her voice. 'Here, Swampy!'

Mother stopped banging and yelling, but Swampy didn't appear – and that *was* unusual. If there's one thing Swampy simply can't resist, it's a full bowl of food. Even Mother started to look rather concerned now.

She looked even more concerned after Dilly spent the rest of the day in the garden calling for

Swampy, without success. There was simply no sign of the little swamp lizard anywhere. At bedtime, Dilly was near to tears.

'Swampy *will* be back tomorrow, won't he, Mother?' he said. He was sitting in his bed, hugging an old blanket from the bottom of Swampy's basket. 'I mean, he's probably just got lost or something, hasn't he?'

'Er . . . I should think so, Dilly,' Mother replied, and kissed him on his snout. 'You go to sleep now. I'm, er . . . sure everything will be all right.'

I could tell Mother didn't really believe that, and judging by the grim expression on Father's face, neither did he. Dilly gripped Swampy's blanket more tightly, slid down under the covers, and closed his eyes.

Swampy didn't come in through his flap that night, and hadn't appeared by lunch-time the next day. Dilly was in a real state, and asked Mother and Father over and over again what they thought had happened to his pet.

'Ah . . .' said father uneasily at last, with a glance at Mother. 'That's something we don't really know as yet, Dilly. Swampy could be OK, of course, but I think you ought not to, er . . . get your hopes up too high . . .'

'I'm afraid your father's right, Dilly,' Mother added in her It's-Awful-But-You've-Got-To-Be-Strong tone of voice. 'It's dangerous for swamp lizards out there. The traffic in this neighbourhood is terrible these days . . .'

Dilly stood listening to them, and looked rather puzzled now, as well as worried. Mother and Father were obviously trying to get him used to the idea that Swampy might *never* come back – but it wasn't working.

'What they *mean*, Dilly,' I said, 'is that they think Swampy's been run over. You know, hit by a dino-car, flattened, D-E-A-D, dead. Got it?'

Dilly got it all right. He stared at me in horror for a second . . . then, you guessed it, he opened his mouth and fired off an ultra-special, 150-mile-per-hour super-scream, the kind that shows us just how upset he is.

Mother and Father were pretty upset too – with *me*. Once Dilly stopped screaming and they'd recovered, they gave me quite a telling off. Dilly sobbed in the background while I did my best to defend myself.

'Well, I don't think what you said *was* very

helpful, Dorla,' whispered Mother. I noticed Dilly's sobs had suddenly subsided into silence. 'It's bad enough for your little brother that his pet should be, er . . . without you, er . . .'

'But he *isn't*, Mother,' said Dilly quietly. Mother, Father and I turned round. Now Dilly was standing with his fists clenched, and an expression of utter certainty on his face. 'I've decided Swampy *has* to be alive.'

'Listen, Dilly,' said Mother gently. 'I think you need to be a bit more realistic about this. In all the time you've had him, Swampy's never been missing this long, has he? We're only preparing you for the worst.'

'But I don't want you to, Mother,' he said. 'I

want you to help me look for him instead. Can't we do a proper search, like on those TV crime shows? We could ask everybody in the street if they've seen him.'

'I don't know, Dilly,' said Father. 'I doubt if anyone would have . . .'

'And it might be *very* upsetting, Dilly,' said Mother. 'I wouldn't . . .'

Dilly narrowed his eyes, opened his mouth, and got ready to deliver another super-scream. I dived behind the sofa . . . but it was OK. Mother and Father held up their paws, and surrendered immediately.

'We'd better get our coats, dear,' sighed Father. 'You too, Dorla.'

Dilly closed his mouth with a SNAP! and headed for the front door, determination in every stride. And within half an hour, we had spoken to each of our neighbours, except old Mr Darma, who was on holiday.

None of them had seen Swampy.

'I'm sorry, Dilly,' said Mother. She and Father had spent most of the time keeping Dilly away from the kerb, in case he spotted a splattered Swampy in the gutter, I suppose. 'I know it's very hard to accept, but . . .'

'*You* can do what ever you like, Mother,' muttered Dilly fiercely as we went back through our front door. 'But I'm not accepting *anything*. I've got another idea, and this one is bound to work, I'm absolutely sure of it . . .'

That afternoon, Dilly produced a special poster. At the top he put in big letters: URGENT. HAVE YOU SEEN THIS SWAMP LIZARD? Beneath that was a picture of Swampy, and our dino-phone number and address.

Dilly made Father go to the Shopping Cavern to have copies made, and then we went out again to pin them up on fences, billboards and fern trees all over the neighbourhood. It was nearly dark when we finished.

'You certainly have to give him credit,' I heard Father saying later that evening, after Dilly had gone to bed. 'He doesn't give up easily.'

The next morning, we were eating breakfast . . . when suddenly there was a knock on the front door. Dilly ran to open it, and there was the dinosaur who delivers our letters, holding one of Dilly's posters in his paw.

'Hi, there!' he said. 'I think I might be able to help you. I'm pretty sure I saw your swamp lizard, er . . . three days ago. And if my memory serves me right, he was slipping under the fence into Mr Darma's garden, and . . .'

Dilly was off before the post-dinosaur had even finished speaking.

To cut a long story short, we found Swampy in Mr Darma's shed. Mr Darma must have left the shed door open. It seems Swampy had gone in for a sleep, and the wind had blown the door shut, trapping him inside.

Anyway, he and Dilly were *very* happy to have found each other again.

'Er . . . I think we owe you an apology, Dilly,' said Mother as we were walking home. Dilly was carrying Swampy, and having his whole face licked frantically by his wriggling pet. 'We should have listened to you.'

'It doesn't matter, Mother,' said Dilly. 'Besides, I was only doing what you and Father used to say,' he added, rolling his eyes. 'You know, all that stuff about being able to achieve anything if you really set your mind to it.'

Then he put Swampy down, and the two of them ran on ahead.

Mother and Father stood with their mouths open for a second.

'He's right,' said Mother at last. 'We *did* use to say that, didn't we?'

'Well, maybe we ought to start saying it again . . .' said Father.

Then we all looked at each other – and set off in the same direction as Dilly and Swampy. Suddenly, Mother and Father had more of a spring in their step. And I just couldn't wait for that tail-ball tournament to begin . . .

A few weeks later, after my team had easily won the tournament, and Mother had got the job, and the summer fair had been a terrific success, Father insisted that we all go out for a family celebration at MacDinosaurs.

'What would we do without you, Dilly?' said Mother on the way there.

Dilly gave her a funny look. But for once . . . I simply had to agree!

3 Dilly breaks the rules

One day a few weeks ago, I was just coming out of the sitting-room when I spotted Father walking across the hall. He glanced into the kitchen as he went past, and stopped suddenly – so I guessed something was wrong.

'Hold it right there, Dilly!' Father said, crossly. I sneaked over and tried to look round him, but he filled most of the doorway. 'You know you're not allowed to eat any of those without asking first. It's against the rules.'

I pushed my head between Father's leg and the doorframe . . . and saw Dilly frozen in mid-crime. He was on a chair by the counter, his paw deep inside the fern-cookie jar. His snout was covered with crumbs as well.

Dilly has been very naughty recently, and it's been getting on Father's nerves. Earlier that morning I'd heard Father talking to Mother about what they should do. Neither of them seemed to have any answers, though.

'But I was hungry,' Dilly replied, sulkily. Then he squared his shoulders, puffed out his chest, and gave Father a defiant stare. 'Anyway, *how* do I know what's against all your rules? They're not written down, are they?'

'You're right, they're not,' said Father in a strange tone of voice – and paused. 'Umm . . . perhaps . . .' he murmured at last. 'Yes . . . it might work. Thanks, Dilly. You've given me a *terrific* idea!'

'I have?' said Dilly, carefully easing his paw from the jar and screwing its lid back on. He flashed Father that cheesy, Actually-I'm-Such-A-Good-Little-Dinosaur grin of his. 'Er . . . does that mean you're . . . letting me off?'

'As if,' said Father.

Dilly's grin vanished.

'You can go to your room and stay there until supper. Provided your big sister doesn't keep us blocking the doorway for ever, that is. Don't *you* have anything better to do, Dorla?'

I pulled my head free, but Father didn't bother to wait for an answer. He strode towards the study, whistling a happy tune. Dilly emerged from the kitchen and made a horrible Yah-Boo-Sucks face in

Father's direction.

'Huh . . . adults!' grunted Dilly. 'What was *that* all about?'

'Search me,' I said. I had a feeling we'd find out soon enough, though . . .

One evening a few days later, Father got up from the table straight after dinner and cleared a space in the magnets on the fridge door. He placed a sheet of paper there, fixed a magnet in each corner, then turned round.

'Ahem . . . could I have your attention, please, Dilly?' said Father. Mother, Dilly and I were still sitting in our seats. Father stood by the fridge with a wooden spoon in his paw. 'I've got something I want to show you.'

'Wow, cool, Father!' said Dilly eagerly. 'Have

you bought me a present?'

'No, Dilly,' said Father with a deep sigh. 'Do you remember what you said about the rules not being written down? Well, they are now.'

Father used the spoon to point at the rules as he read them out. Each was numbered, and they were very simple. **Rule 1:** *No screaming*. **Rule 2:** *No stamping or slamming doors*. **Rule 3:** *No name calling*, and so on . . .

'You don't look impressed, Dilly,' said Mother, who seemed amused.

'I'm *not*,' snapped Dilly. 'Can I go and watch TV?'

'Of course,' said Father. Dilly jumped off his chair and raised his foot. 'Er, Rule 2, Dilly . . .' Father growled in his Don't-You-Dare voice. Dilly lowered his foot gently. 'There you are,' Father said. 'It's easy, isn't it?'

Dilly didn't reply, but simply turned on his heel and grumpily walked away. A broad smile spread slowly across Father's face. As Mother said later, he hasn't looked *that* cheerful since Dino-Town United won the Cup.

He stayed cheerful for the next couple of days, too. Every time Dilly did anything naughty and tried to argue about it, Father just pointed at a rule on the fridge door list, or referred to the copy of it he kept in his pocket.

Soon Father only had to say, 'Rule 4, Dilly!' from behind his newspaper or, 'Rule 8!' and Dilly would freeze on the spot before he could even start misbehaving. As you can imagine, Father thought this was *marvellous*.

Dilly *had* to be good – and he became more and more frustrated. He did a lot of muttering, but there didn't seem to be anything else he could do. Then, that weekend, Grandmother and Grandfather came to visit us.

'OK, who's for a hot cup of fern-leaf tea and a nice slice of marsh-mud pie?' asked Mother when they arrived. We were in the sitting-room, and Father was in the hall, hanging up their coats. 'I made it fresh this morning.'

'Great, count me in,' said Grandfather. 'It's my favourite!'

'Do you really think that's wise, dear?' said Grandmother, giving him a stern look. 'Your diet's been going so well, and I thought the rule was . . .'

'Oh, fiddlesticks,' said Grandfather. 'Every rule has an exception, and I've decided today's is marsh-mud pie! Make mine a *large* slice, OK?'

Mother and I laughed – but Dilly didn't. I noticed he went quiet instead, and I realised something had begun to brew in his devious little mind . . .

Grandmother and Grandfather left eventually, and then it was bath and bed time. Dilly didn't make his usual fuss ('Rule 7, Dilly!'), and I read for a while before I fell asleep. But I was wide awake again before long.

That's right, you guessed it . . . Dilly was letting loose an ultra-special, 150-mile-per-hour super-scream, the kind that brings Mother and Father dashing to see what's happened. I followed them into his room.

Dilly's scream stopped *instantly*. It was almost as if he'd turned it off with a switch. He was sitting up in bed, and for a second I thought he might be

smiling. But the light wasn't on, and it was hard to be certain.

'Right, Dilly,' said Father, who had his arms folded and was tapping his foot, so I knew he thought Dilly was being deliberately naughty. 'Would you care to explain exactly why you've broken Rule 1? I'm waiting.'

'I was having a terrible nightmare, Father,' said Dilly, wiping a tear from his eye, and giving a little sniff. 'Then suddenly I woke up, it was dark – and I screamed to get you and Mother here. I didn't think you'd mind.'

'Ah, I see,' said Father. 'Under the circumstances, I suppose . . .'

'So could we make that an exception to the rule?' Dilly asked quickly. 'I mean, shouldn't Rule 1 be – no screaming . . . *unless I'm frightened and I need to attract your attention very fast*? Or something like that, anyway.'

'He does have a point, you know,' said Mother.

'OK, OK,' said Father irritably. 'We'll change it tomorrow.'

There was no mistaking the smile on Dilly's face as Mother tucked him in, even if the light in his bedroom was still off. And, first thing the next morning, he made Father take down the list of rules and add the exception.

There were plenty more to come. That day, every time Father said, 'Rule 5!' or 'Rule 9!' Dilly would stop what he was doing, think for a moment, then come up with a reason why this particular occasion was an exception.

He was pretty good at it, as well. Take Rule 2, for example.

'I *know* I was STAMPING, Father,' he said in the garden that afternoon. 'But a nasty creepy-crawly was trying to bite me. And I had to SLAM the back door when I ran in because it won't shut otherwise. Tell him, Dorla.'

'It's true, Father,' I said. 'Didn't Mother ask you to mend it?'

'Er . . . never mind that,' Father blustered. 'Well, what about Rule 3, then?' he said, confidently. 'I distinctly heard you calling your sister names.'

'OK, I admit it,' said Dilly, and Father's face immediately took on a Hah-I-Thought-So! expression. 'But we were playing dino-pirates, Father,' said Dilly. 'And I only called her a filthy buccaneer. That wasn't rude, was it?'

Father was scowling as he changed Rule 3 to read: no name calling . . . *unless it's part of a game (and not rude)*. Dilly watched him put the list of rules back on the fridge door, then skipped off whistling a happy tune.

After that, things began to get difficult. It was soon obvious Dilly was working his way down the list, breaking each rule in order, so he could argue with Father about it. Mother said it had become a battle of wills.

The list steadily got more and more scribbled on and messy, with lots of crossings-out and

arrows and underlinings. Then, one day, I was there when Father caught Dilly with his paw inside the fern-cookie jar again.

And this time Father refused point blank to accept Dilly's exception.

'Rule 13 clearly states *no fern cookies without asking first*, Dilly,' he said in a stern, clipped voice. 'I don't care if you *were* starving because you gave your lunch to Swampy, you're still grounded for . . . for a week!'

'Hey, that's *so* unfair,' squealed Dilly. I noticed he seemed to be hiding something behind him. 'Last time I got told off for this you only sent me to my room until supper. *I* think there ought to be rules for grown-ups, too!'

'I don't know about that,' spluttered Father. 'I'd have to see them first . . .'

'No problem, Father,' said Dilly. He whipped out a scribbled-on toilet roll and let it unspool across the floor. '**Rule 1:** *No unfair punishments,*' he read out. '**Rule 2:** *No unnecessary shouting.* **Rule 3:** *No favourites . . .*'

Father listened as Dilly went steadily through his entire list. Father opened his mouth once or twice, almost as if he had thought of some exceptions to Dilly's rules . . . but each time he closed it again, silently.

'OK, Dilly,' he said at last, with a big sigh. 'What do I have to do?'

'Simple,' said Dilly. 'You tear up your list, and I'll tear up mine.'

Father glanced wistfully at the fridge door for a second . . . then smiled.

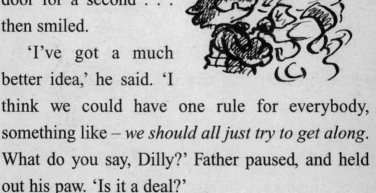

'I've got a much better idea,' he said. 'I think we could have one rule for everybody, something like – *we should all just try to get along.* What do you say, Dilly?' Father paused, and held out his paw. 'Is it a deal?'

'Er . . . OK,' said Dilly, shaking Father's paw. 'Anything for a quiet life.'

No chance of *that*, I thought. But I didn't say a word . . .

4 Dilly and the book of bad behaviour

'YIPPEEEEEEE!' yelled Dilly as he burst into the kitchen. Mother jumped and spilled swamp juice down her front, and Father nearly choked on his fern flakes. 'It's . . . CHRISTMAS!' Dilly added, racing round the table.

'Actually – it isn't,' I said, calmly continuing with my breakfast. Dilly had begun to sing *Bronto Bells* at the top of his voice. 'Not yet, anyway.'

'Dorla's right, Dilly,' said Mother, dabbing

crossly at the stain on her top. 'It's November, so there's more than a month to go. Now will you PLEASE stop running around like that! You're making me feel dizzy.'

'Sorry, Mother,' said Dilly breathlessly, skidding to a halt. He bumped into the table and made Father's swamp juice topple over. 'But Christmas is coming, isn't it? And I'm going to get *loads* of presents! I'm so excited . . .'

'Huh, you'd never guess, would you?' I muttered, buttering a fern stalk.

Everybody loves Christmas, but Dilly is totally obsessed with it. He started on about it almost as soon as we got back from our holiday – in August!

And for the last few days he's hardly mentioned anything else.

'Er . . . I think it's time we had a talk on that subject, Dilly,' said Father, desperately trying to prevent a stream of sticky swamp juice dripping on to the floor, and failing. 'Now we *all* want a happy Christmas, don't we?'

'Which means we don't want it spoiled by you being naughty,' said Mother. 'You know what you're like, Dilly. The more excited you get, the worse you behave, and you're very excited already. You just said so.'

'And don't forget, Dino Claus only visits *good* little dinosaurs,' added Father. 'He writes down the names of the naughty ones in his Book of Bad Behaviour, and if your name's in it . . . *you won't get any presents*.'

Dilly looked at Mother and Father and gulped nervously. Then his face took on a familiar, crafty expression, and I realised he wasn't convinced.

'But how does Dino Claus know if you've been naughty?' he asked. 'You said he lives in the middle of the Great Swamp and doesn't leave, except when he delivers everybody's presents on Christmas Eve.'

'Oh, that's easy,' said Mother, with a smile. 'It's . . . *magic*.'

Dilly's crafty expression vanished instantly, and his shoulders slumped. Mother had given him the perfect answer. If you believe in Dino Claus – and Dilly does, deeply – then there was simply no arguing with *that*.

They all seemed to have forgotten Dino Claus visits the Shopping Cavern every year before Christmas. He collects money for charity, and you can meet him. At the time, there seemed no reason to remind them.

'Don't look so worried, Dilly,' said Father. 'As far as I'm aware, Dino Claus only starts to write names in his book after . . . well, after the middle of November. You just have to be good from, er . . . today until Christmas.'

'But . . . but I'm not sure I can be, Father,' said Dilly, frowning.

'Nonsense!' said Mother, briskly. 'Just keep yourself under control, Dilly. Don't get over-excited, and you'll be fine. Now, eat your breakfast.'

'OK, Mother,' said Dilly uncertainly – and did as he was told.

I saw Mother and Father exchange hopeful glances. They looked pretty pleased with themselves, and I had to admit using the Book of Bad Behaviour seemed like a neat wheeze. Maybe their best ever, I thought.

Of course, their cunning little schemes never turn out quite as they expect, so I realised they might need some help. They generally do . . .

Dilly behaved himself for the rest of that day, and the day after, and the day after that. As November passed into December, he was *still* being good. And, incredibly, he didn't talk about Christmas – not even *once*.

I don't think Mother and Father could believe it at first, but gradually they began to relax. The moment came when they seemed to think it was safe to mention Christmas again. We were at the table, having dinner.

'Dorla and I are going to write out some Christmas cards this evening, Dilly,' said Mother brightly. 'And we, er . . . wondered if you wanted to help. You'd better let us know how many you'll need for your friends, too.'

Silence fell across the table as the three of us waited for Dilly to reply. But something peculiar was happening to him. His eyes were rolling, his body was quivering, and his fists were clenched round his knife and fork.

The quivering grew worse, the handles of his knife and fork kept banging on the table, and for a second it looked as though he might even EXPLODE! Then his face took on a strange, tortured expression . . .

And suddenly he went very, very still.

'I don't think so, Mother,' he murmured at last in a small, strangled voice. His eyes had stopped rolling, and he was staring dead ahead now. 'I won't be needing cards this year, either. I'm . . . not . . . giving . . . any.'

He uttered the last four words through gritted teeth.

I was amazed. Usually Dilly is *desperate* to help with the cards, and he always gives lots to his friends. Last year he gave Dixie *seventeen*. I think Mother and Father were more worried about his health, though.

'Are you all right, Dilly?' said Mother anxiously, leaning across and putting a paw on his forehead. 'You haven't got a temperature . . .'

'I'm fine, Mother,' said Dilly more normally. 'I was just keeping myself under control. You know, so I won't get over-excited. I don't want my name to end up in Dino Claus's Book of Bad Behaviour, do I?'

'Er . . . no, I suppose not,' said Mother, slightly taken aback.

'It's hard, though,' said Dilly. 'I just have to hear the word Chri . . . that word, and I can feel myself starting to get excited. Maybe it's best if no one mentions it in front of me until the Big Day. Is that OK?'

'Are you sure, Dilly?' said Father uncertainly.

'Absolutely, Father,' said Dilly decisively. 'It's the only way.'

Mother and Father glanced at each other . . . and shrugged. From then on, they did what Dilly wanted, and avoided the subject of Christmas when he was around. And Dilly's unbelievable run of good behaviour continued.

But if you think that made Mother and Father happy, you'd be wrong. Pretty soon they were looking rather *un*happy, and I didn't feel particularly cheerful myself. Christmas wasn't turning out to be much fun this year.

'It's not fair, Mother,' I whispered at bedtime one evening. Dilly was in his room, but I had to whisper in case he overheard the dreaded word. 'Not mentioning Christmas means *none* of us can get into the spirit.'

'I know,' sighed Mother. 'Don't worry. We'll think of something.'

Needless to say . . . they didn't. In fact, with only two weeks to go, they still hadn't bought a Christmas Fern – and all because of Dilly. So I simply sulked till they did. Dilly would have to put up with it, I said.

After that, he wouldn't go in the sitting-room, or even *look* in there.

'Listen, Dilly,' Father finally said one day. I thought he sounded a little . . . guilty. 'Your mother and I just want to let you know we don't mind if you, er . . . get over-excited and a bit naughty. After all, it is Christmas.'

Dilly twitched and clenched his fists.

'But . . . you're . . . not . . . the . . . ones . . . who . . . are . . . important,' he muttered through gritted teeth. 'It's . . . Dino . . . Claus . . . and . . . his . . . Book . . . of . . . Bad . . . Behaviour . . . that . . . count . . . I . . . can't . . . take . . . the . . . risk . . . Father.'

Then he stomped stiffly away – STOMP, STOMP, STOMP.

'Oh, terrific,' said Mother once he'd gone. 'Only Dino Claus himself could save us now – and somehow I don't think that's going to happen.'

Things were looking very grim, and I realised the moment for me to step in had definitely arrived. Luckily, Mother had given me an idea.

'We could always ask him,' I said. Mother and Father turned and stared at me with puzzled expressions. 'Dino Claus will be at the Shopping Cavern tomorrow, and this is what I think we should do . . .'

'Dorla, you're a genius!' they said when I'd told them my plan. They hugged me, and though I say so myself, my plan was *fiendishly* clever.

The next day, we were at the head of the queue to meet Dino Claus. Father slipped into the grotto to chat with him first, as I'd suggested, then signalled the rest of us to come in. Dilly was quivering from top to tail.

Dino Claus greeted us with, 'Merry Christmas!' and asked our names.

'Umm, let me see,' said Dino Claus, picking up

a large notebook and flicking through it. 'No, neither of you are in my Book of Bad Behaviour, and I won't be writing any more names in it before Christmas *this* year.'

He winked at me, and I winked back. He'd played his role to perfection.

'Hang on,' said Dilly. 'That means I don't . . . have . . . to . . .' His voice trailed away.

Suddenly, his face took on a look of huge relief, and he fired off an ultra-special, 150-mile-per-hour super-scream . . . of total joy. Then he dashed out as if he had some serious catching up to do.

Mother ran after him, and we could hear crashes in the distance, and Dilly yelling, 'Yippeeeeeeee!

It's . . . CHRISTMAS!' The interior of the grotto was wrecked, and Father apologised, but Dino Claus just laughed.

'Ho, ho, ho! Not to worry,' he boomed. 'Excitement, small dinosaurs letting off steam – it's all part of the magic of Christmas. Now, ahem, I distinctly remember you said something about a contribution to charity . . .'

'I did, didn't I?' said Father with a resigned smile. Then he put a *lot* of money in the charity box. 'There you go, and, er . . . thanks for everything.'

After that we had a fantastic time. Of course,

Dilly was his usual, badly behaved self. But what did it matter? As Mother and Father said . . . A little naughtiness is a small price to pay for a happy Christmas!